A Nature Walk
on the Beach

Louise and Richard Spilsbury

Raintree

Raintree is an imprint of Capstone Global Library Limited, a company incorporated in England and Wales having its registered office at 7 Pilgrim Street, London, EC4V 6LB – Registered company number: 6695582

www.raintreepublishers.co.uk
myorders@raintreepublishers.co.uk

Edited by Joanna Issa, Penny West, Krissy Mohn, and Gina Kammer
Designed by Cynthia Akiyoshi
Picture research by Elizabeth Alexander and Tracy Cummins
Production by Helen McCreath
Originated by Capstone Global Library Ltd
Printed and bound in China by Leo Paper Group

ISBN 978 1 406 28216 0
18 17 16 15 14
10 9 8 7 6 5 4 3 2 1

British Library Cataloguing in Publication Data
A full catalogue record for this book is available from the British Library.

Acknowledgements
We would like to thank the following for permission to reproduce photographs:

Alamy: © George H.H. Huey, front cover, © Malcolm Schuyl, 13; Corbis: © jf/cultura, 20; FLPA: © B. Borrell Casals, 15, © Christiana Carvalho, 7, © ImageBroker, 5, © Phil McLean, 14, © Robin Chittenden, 10, © Steve Trewhella, 11, 18; Shutterstock: Bill Frische, 8, Dimos, 19, Dmitry Fischer, design element (water), Ekaterina Pokrovsky, 12, back cover left, Eric Isselee, design element (Bird), (rabbit), Francisco Caravana, 4, Johannes Kornelius, design element (sand), Kletr, design element (fish), (starfish), Mark Bridger, 21, Matthew Gough, 17, back cover right, Nadiia Korol, 22 top left, Oleksiy Mark, 22 bottom left, romrf, 22 bottom right, Scorpp, design element (shell), Steven Maltby, 16, Subbotina Anna, design element (sea horse), T Cassidy, 22 top right, Vangert, front cover, back cover, design element (crab), Wolfgang Kruck, 6; SuperStock: Minden Pictures, 9.

We would like to thank Michael Bright for his invaluable help in the preparation of this book.

Every effort has been made to contact copyright holders of material reproduced in this book. Any omissions will be rectified in subsequent printings if notice is given to the publisher.

All the Internet addresses (URLs) given in this book were valid at the time of going to press. However, due to the dynamic nature of the Internet, some addresses may have changed, or sites may have changed or ceased to exist since publication. While the author and publisher regret any inconvenience this may cause readers, no responsibility for any such changes can be accepted by either the author or the publisher.

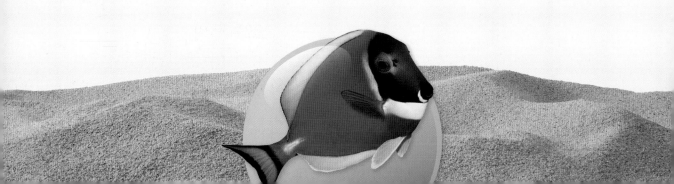

Contents

Some words are shown in bold, **like this**. You can find out what they mean by looking in the glossary.

Where are we going?

We are going to the beach! A beach is a place where the land meets the sea. We are going on a nature walk to spot some amazing plants and animals there.

It can be sunny, windy, and wet at the beach.
Bring a sun hat, coat, and rubber boots.
Choose clothes that do not rustle when you
move, so they do not scare away wildlife.

What is up on the cliffs?

Look up at the cliffs through your binoculars. Can you see gulls in their **nests** made of grass, seaweed, and mud? Most birds lay eggs up high to keep them safe from **predators**.

Guillemots lay their eggs on the edge of the cliff. The eggs are shaped like pears, so they roll in circles and do not fall off.

What can you see in sand dunes?

The plant you can see with lots of long leaves is marram grass. Its **roots** trap sand and help to form the hills we call dunes.

Droppings and tufts of fur outside holes in the sand tell us these holes are rabbit **burrows**. Rabbits make burrows in dunes because sand is easy to dig. They come out to eat grass.

What is on the strand line?

The strand line is where high **tides** wash up waste and dead seaweed. Can you find any dogfish egg cases? These tough, leathery cases protect baby dogfish until they are born.

Use a stick to lift some of the waste. Can you see tiny sand fleas jumping about? They eat rotting seaweed left behind by the tide and then hide under the sand.

What are those lumps on the sand?

Look down at the beach as you walk slowly towards the sea. Can you spot strange coils of sand on the surface? What do you think they are?

lugworm

Lugworms swallow sand underground and take food from it. Then they squeeze the sand out of their bodies in coils at the surface. Hungry birds try to eat lugworms!

Can you spot rings on the rocks?

Look through your magnifying glass at ring-shaped grooves on the rocks. These are called scars. The scars tell us about an animal that lives here. What do you think made them?

scars

After a limpet moves about to feed on seaweed, it goes back to the same spot. The edge of its shell wears a groove in the rock that helps it to stick on tightly.

What lives in rock pools?

Use your nature spotter's guide to help you name the different sea creatures you see in rock pools. Sea anemones have long **tentacles** to sting tiny fish. Then they eat them.

There are hundreds of little tubes under a starfish's arms. These take turns sucking on to rocks to help the starfish move. They also help the starfish open shells, so it can eat the animals inside the shells.

Can you spot some seaweed?

Can you find seaweed in the shallow sea? Look for parts called **holdfasts** at the bottom of the seaweed. These cling to the rocks to stop waves from washing seaweed away.

frond

Bladderwrack seaweed has bubbles of
air on its **fronds**. This helps the fronds to
float near the water's surface to get light.
Seaweed uses light to make food.

How can I protect beaches?

Did you enjoy your nature walk? Protect beaches and their wildlife by picking up litter and cleaning up any dog mess. Maybe you could help with a beach clean-up, too.

Try not to disturb animals living at the beach, and do not step on or pick wildflowers. If you protect beaches, you might see even more wildlife on your next nature walk.

Exploring nature

These things will help you explore the beach on a nature walk.

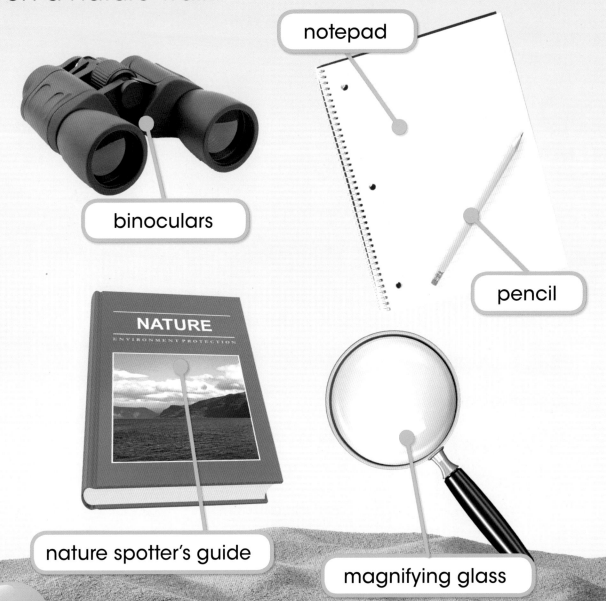

notepad

binoculars

pencil

nature spotter's guide

magnifying glass

Glossary

burrow hole or tunnel dug by a small animal to live in

frond leaf-like part on seaweed

holdfast part of a seaweed that holds it on to rocks

nest place where an animal has its babies

predator animal that catches and eats other animals

root part of a plant that usually grows underground

tentacles long, thin body parts used for touching or stinging

tide high tide is when water comes up a beach; at low tide it goes out again

Find out more

Books

By the Sea (Nature Walks), Clare Collinson (Franklin Watts, 2010)

RSPB Handbook of the Seashore, Maya Plass (A&C Black Publishers Ltd, 2013)

Seashores (Nature Trails), Anita Ganeri (Raintree, 2011)

Websites

www.rnli.org/safetyandeducation/stayingsafe/beach-safety/Pages/Beach-safety-advice.aspx

Follow this advice from the RNLI to stay safe on the beach.

www.sciencemuseum.org.uk/onlinestuff/snot/where_does_all_the_water_go_at_low_tide.aspx

Visit this website to learn how tides work.

Index